THE
B.L.E.S.S.
FAMILY RESOURCE

Developed by Lisa Ferguson

A resource for families based on the book *B.L.E.S.S.: 5 Everyday Ways To Love Your Neighbor and Change the World* by Dave Ferguson and Jon Ferguson

Sonburst, LLC
Chicago, Illinois
www.sonburst.info

ISBN: 979-8-9885828-0-9

Published in the United States by

Sonburst, LLC
Chicago, IL
www.sonburst.info
sonburstinfo@gmail.com

Edited by Lindy Lowry

Designed by Lena Roberson (lenaroberson.com)

For information on discounted bulk orders for non-profits, please visit our website: www.sonburst.info.

A letter to parents

Dear Parents,

I'm thrilled you've picked up *The B.L.E.S.S. Family Resource*! I've prayed that you and your family will embark on a wonderful journey as you experience it together.

Like you, my husband and I knew it was our responsibility to lead our children to faith in Jesus. We wanted to follow God's instructions to families in Deuteronomy chapter 6 to reach their hearts, as well as their minds, and encourage them to put their learning into practice every day. And we made many attempts to do this—from bedtime Bible readings, to morning devotions, to Bible verses we kept in a small box on our kitchen table.

But regardless of the resources we bought or borrowed, none were really effective in helping us keep the Bible stories alive in our home after the reading.

Thanks to my education and experience in the field of early childhood, I understood that our children were likely still pondering the Bible stories a few days after hearing them. And on a few occasions, we were blessed to discover this! I was also aware that hearing the stories more than once was necessary for them to develop a deeper understanding of the text. I recognized the importance of engaging them in thoughtful conversations where they felt heard and understood, and where Jon and I could share authentically too (and appropriately for their ages). And I knew they needed to make sense of the stories in ways that were meaningful to them. I was confident that all these components were necessary to build not only our children's active faith, but Jon's and mine as well. And yet we never found a resource that included everything we were looking for to disciple our young family.

Fast-forward several years …

Our children are now young adults, but I never stopped wrestling with this issue for other families. That's why I'm so excited you've found *The B.L.E.S.S. Family Resource*. I've written it with you and your family in mind. It's the kind of resource we wish we'd had when our children were young. I pray it will bless you and your family and inspire you to keep B.L.E.S.S.ing others long after you close this resource!

Blessings to you!

Lisa

WELCOME

I'm excited for you and your family to use *The B.L.E.S.S. Family Resource* to discover and put into practice the "five everyday ways to love your neighbor and change the world" based on the book *B.L.E.S.S.* by Dave Ferguson and Jon Ferguson.

This resource includes five B.L.E.S.S. Practice Toolkits. Each Toolkit focuses on one B.L.E.S.S. practice and Bible story that correspond to those included in the book *B.L.E.S.S.* Each Toolkit also includes fun and practical ideas to keep the B.L.E.S.S. practices and Bible stories alive in your home and encourage your family to be on mission to bless others in Jesus' name.

Choose from four great ways to use this family resource:

- *6-Week Plan for Individual Families*
- *21-Week Plan for Individual Families*
- *6-Week Plan for Small Groups of Families*
- *21-Week Plan for Small Groups of Families*

Get the *B.L.E.S.S.* book

If you'd like to purchase the book *B.L.E.S.S.: 5 Everyday Ways To Love Your Neighbor and Change the World,* visit **bless-book.org**.

THE B.L.E.S.S. FAMILY RESOURCE
INSIDE

"'Love the Lord your God with all your heart and with all your soul and with all your mind.' This is the first and greatest commandment. And the second is like it: 'Love your neighbor as yourself.'"

MATTHEW 22:37-39 (NIV)

CONVERSATION GUIDE

Using the Conversation Guide, choose a day early in the week when your family will not be rushed to read the Bible story aloud and engage your family in a thought-provoking conversation around the B.L.E.S.S. practice. Make it a special time and encourage everyone to get comfy and cozy. The "Warm-Up" question (each person should answer it briefly) sets the stage for the reading. Ask everyone to listen carefully to see how the question connects to the Bible story. The "Reflect" questions (which focus on the Bible story) and "Apply" questions (which apply the reading to real-life situations) serve as springboards to generate meaningful conversation, beyond simply answering the questions. Choose as many or as few as you'd like, but make sure you begin with the Reflection section before moving on to the Apply questions. Be sure to take cues from your children—if they seem tired or restless, you can always stop and return to where you left off on another day. Use the "Wrap up" at the end of each Toolkit to summarize your conversation and then finish with prayer: each person can pray or one person can pray for the whole family.

BIBLE STORY

Each B.L.E.S.S. practice focuses on a different Bible story that corresponds with those included in the book *B.L.E.S.S.* For this resource, the Bible stories were adapted to be easy to read and understand. Placing the resource in an open Bible as you read will help children connect the stories to the actual Bible. Follow the Conversation Guide to begin and end each reading. If you'd like to read the Bible story more than once, use the additional Conversations Guides (First Impressions and Reflections) at the back of this resource for the first and final readings. There are so many benefits to hearing a story read aloud, even for children who already know how to read. So consider reading the story aloud each time and encouraging your children to sit back, relax and imagine the scenes in their minds as they listen.

MEMORY VERSE

We've included a key Bible verse related to each B.L.E.S.S. practice and corresponding Bible story with suggestions for motions to help your whole family memorize it. Recite it together after reading the Bible story with the Conversation Guide, and then make it a part of your daily routine, such as before a meal, at bedtime or on your way to school. Find fun and creative ways to change it up. For example, take turns saying each word or phrase until the end. Or pause now and then to let someone else say the next word.

TABLE TALK

These questions are meant to help you engage in casual conversations over a meal or dessert to keep the B.L.E.S.S. practices and Bible stories alive in your home. Choose one question for everyone (parents too!) to answer. For added fun, ask someone to choose a number (1 to 8), then read the corresponding question aloud. Encourage everyone to respond to what is shared with comments and questions to get a genuine conversation going.

TOGETHER TIME

A variety of ideas are included to help you integrate the B.L.E.S.S. practice and corresponding Bible story into your family's daily routines and experiences in fun and practical ways, including opportunities to serve together. Some of the activities can be repeated while others will be one-time events. Read these in advance to decide which activity you'll try and when, and then make plans as necessary. Have fun being on mission together to B.L.E.S.S. others!

For more helpful tips,
visit www.sonburst.info.

BEGIN WITH PRAYER

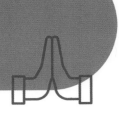

CONVERSATION GUIDE

Ask a "Warm-Up" question

If you could stay up all night doing just one thing, what would it be?

Read the Bible story

Before you read, pray out loud to invite the Holy Spirit's presence. Then encourage everyone to imagine the scenes in the story as they listen.

After you read, ask how the Warm-Up question connected to the Bible story. *(Jesus prayed all night.)*

Talk about it

Use the questions below as springboards for conversation. Choose from the Reflect questions first, and then from the Apply questions.

REFLECT

- Why do you think it was so important for Jesus to choose good leaders? Besides praying, what else could Jesus have done to make this important decision? What would *you* have done?

- What do you think about Jesus' decision to pray before choosing his leaders? How do you think prayer helped Jesus?

- Why do you think Jesus prayed alone? What do you think about his choice?

- What do you imagine it was like for Jesus to spend the whole night praying on the mountain? Why do you think he prayed outside? All night? What do you think Jesus said in his prayer?

- What do you think Jesus thought about prayer? How do you know?

APPLY

- When you have a big decision to make, what do you usually do first? What can you learn from Jesus' example? What's difficult about this?

- How do you feel knowing you can pray to God by yourself, any time, any place, about anything? How might this help you pray differently?

- How might beginning your morning with prayer make a difference in your day? In the day of someone you're praying for, or we're praying for as a family?

- Share about a time when you or someone you know "began with prayer"—before meeting someone, going somewhere, making a decision, etc. How was prayer helpful?

- How can you "begin with prayer" this week on your own? How can we "begin with prayer" as a family?

Wrap up

Summarize the conversation, restating what you learned about B.L.E.S.S. Practice #1 (*Begin with prayer*) through the Bible story.

Pray

Think of one or two people you know in your neighborhood, family, at school or at work who have yet to follow Jesus. Pray for opportunities to B.L.E.S.S. them. Pray also for the people you don't know yet whom God will put in your path to B.L.E.S.S. throughout this series.

THANK Jesus for being our example of what it means to "begin with prayer."

ASK the Holy Spirit to help you remember to "begin with prayer" so that you'll be aware of ways you can B.L.E.S.S. others throughout the day.

BIBLE STORY

Jesus Chooses The Twelve Apostles

(Matt. 9:35-36; 10:1-4; Mark 1:9-15; 3:7-8, 13-19; Luke 4:1-15; 6:12-16; 8:1-3; 9:1-6)

Adapted from Scripture by Lisa Ferguson

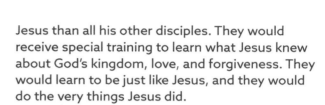

After Jesus was baptized by John the Baptizer in the Jordan River, he was led by the Holy Spirit into the desert where he spent forty days and forty nights fasting and praying. He was preparing for the marvelous, saving work planned since the beginning of creation.

After this time of testing and training, Jesus returned to Galilee in the power of the Holy Spirit. Now he was fully prepared to begin the important, rescuing work he came to do.

At once, Jesus began preaching a message similar to John the Baptizer: "The time has come! The kingdom of God is near! Turn away from your wrong choices and believe the Good News of the kingdom of God!" He went through all the towns and villages, teaching in synagogues, preaching the Good News and healing every disease and sickness.

News of Jesus began to spread. Everywhere he went, large crowds of people gathered around him. Many people followed Jesus and they became known as his disciples. Some were women, including Mary Magdalene, Joanna and Susanna. These women were very generous and supported Jesus' work by paying for what was needed. Others were loyal men who left everything behind to follow Jesus.

When Jesus saw the crowds, he had compassion on them. He knew they were hurting and helpless, like sheep without their shepherd. Jesus knew he would need to select a special group of leaders to share in the work of spreading the Good News of the kingdom of God. These men would spend more time with

Jesus than all his other disciples. They would receive special training to learn what Jesus knew about God's kingdom, love, and forgiveness. They would learn to be just like Jesus, and they would do the very things Jesus did.

When it was finally time to make this decision, Jesus went up to the mountainside alone to pray. He spent the whole night praying to the Father.

In the morning, Jesus called all of his disciples together. One by one, Jesus named his twelve new leaders:

Simon, to whom Jesus gave the name Peter, which means "The Rock," and Peter's brother, Andrew;

James and John, the sons of Zebedee, whom Jesus called "The Sons of Thunder";

Philip;

Bartholomew, also called Nathaniel;

Thomas;

Matthew the tax collector, also known as Levi;

James the Younger, the son of Alphaeus;

Thaddeus, also called Jude;

Simon the Zealot;

and Judas Iscariot, who would later betray Jesus.

Jesus gave these twelve men his authority to drive out evil spirits and to heal every disease and sickness. They were now apostles—messengers prepared by Jesus and then sent by Jesus out into the world to spread the Good News of the kingdom of God to people everywhere!

MEMORY VERSE

"The prayer of a righteous person is powerful and effective."

JAMES 5:16 (NIV)

Involve the whole family in memorizing the Bible verse to keep the B.L.E.S.S. practice and Bible story in your hearts and minds.

NOTE: Help children understand that a "righteous" person is one who believes and follows Jesus.

WORDS	ACTIONS
"The prayer	Praying hands
of a righteous person	Hands over heart
is powerful	Show arm muscles
and effective."	Hit left palm with side of right hand
James 5:16	Form open Bible with both hands

TABLE TALK

During a meal or dessert, choose a question below for everyone to answer.
Encourage everyone to respond to what is shared with comments and questions
to get a conversation going around the B.L.E.S.S practice and Bible story.

☐ Chat 1 What's your earliest memory of prayer? Where were you? With whom? What did you pray about? How did you feel?

☐ Chat 2 Why do you think God wants us to pray? What do you think prayer does for us? What does prayer do for the people we pray for?

☐ Chat 3 Do you prefer to pray by yourself or with others? Why might it be helpful to pray out loud with others? Share your experiences.

☐ Chat 4 If you could go anywhere to pray to God, where would you go? How might the place where we pray make a difference in our prayers?

☐ Chat 5 If someone asked you what it means to pray, how to pray, and what to pray about, what would you say?

☐ Chat 6 Has it ever been difficult for you to pray? Explain. What can we do when it's difficult to pray?

☐ Chat 7 The Bible says that prayer is "powerful and effective." What do you think this means? Share about a time when prayer was "powerful and effective" for you or someone you know.

☐ Chat 8 Share your experiences with "beginning with prayer" this week as a way to bless others. How did this make a difference in your day?

TOGETHER TIME 😄

The following ideas provide opportunities for you to integrate the B.L.E.S.S. practice and Bible story into your family's daily routines and experiences in fun and practical ways. Include the ideas that work best for your family and have fun blessing others together!

Prayer walk

As you walk (or drive) to run errands together, before you enter the store, bank, laundromat, etc., have one person pray for God to use your family to bless the people there. Then look and listen for opportunities to do so!

Loving your neighbors

Before everyone leaves in the morning, stop and pray together at breakfast, at the door, or in the car. Ask God to help each of you watch and listen carefully for an opportunity to bless someone in a meaningful way. Then be on the lookout to see what opportunities emerge throughout the day. Be prepared to share your experiences later when you all return home.

Family outing

Visit the highest point in your community—a hill, mountain, building, or even the highest point on a playground. As you look below, share what you see from this perspective. Take a few minutes to imagine Jesus praying on the mountain for his disciples. Follow Jesus' example and pray for your community below, including the people God is putting in your lives to bless. Enjoy your "mountain top" experience together.

Tower of power

Collect stackable items like flat rocks, small boxes, plastic lids, etc. and non-toxic paint pens. Ask each person to name one or two people whom they would like to bless and draw a simple image on the item to represent them, such as a house to represent a neighbor. (Draw on removable masking tape if you'd like to preserve the items.) Place these in a basket. Before bedtime, ask each person to choose one item and pray out loud for that person. As you find ways to bless these folks, remove their item from the basket and stack them to create a "tower of power" in a prominent place that will remind your family of the power of prayer. At the end of each week, return the items to the basket and begin again. Add more items as you find more people to bless.

Branches of blessings

Take a walk together to collect fallen tree branches. When you get home, put them in a vase in a visible area. Cut old clothes into strips and place them in a basket near the vase. Then plan a special prayer time to kick off the series: ask each person to name one or two people they'd like to bless and then pray for them. For each person they pray for, they can tie one fabric strip to the branches. Throughout this series, add a strip each time you B.L.E.S.S. someone. Have fun counting your blessings!

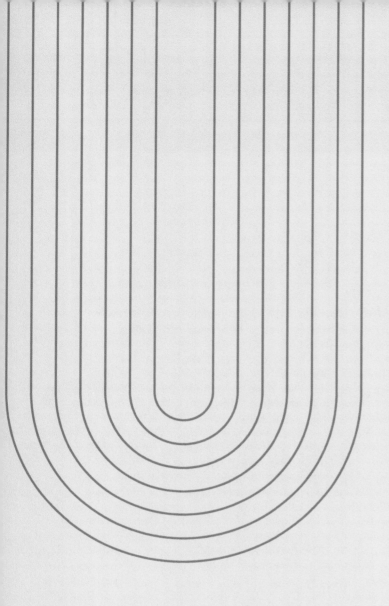

WHAT'S NEXT? ———————————→

B.L.E.S.S. PRACTICE TOOLKIT #2
LISTEN

LISTEN

CONVERSATION GUIDE

Ask a "Warm-Up" question

Who is the best listener in your family?
What makes them such a good listener?

Read the Bible story

Before you read, pray out loud to invite the Holy Spirit's presence. Then encourage everyone to imagine the scenes in the story as they listen.

After you read, ask how the Warm-Up question connected to the Bible story. *(Jesus stopped and listened to Bartimaeus.)*

Talk about it

Use the questions below as springboards for conversation. Choose from the Reflect questions first, and then from the Apply questions.

REFLECT

- Besides being blind, what do you notice about Bartimaeus? What do you think he believed about Jesus? How do you know?

- Why do you think the people told Bartimaeus to be quiet? What do you think about his reaction to their words? What would you have done?

- Why do you think Jesus stopped to listen to Bartimaeus? How do you think Bartimaeus felt about this? How might the crowd have felt?

- What do you think it means to have mercy on someone? Why do you think Bartimaeus asked Jesus to have mercy on him before he asked Jesus to heal him? What did this tell Jesus about Bartimaeus?

- Jesus could see that Bartimaeus was blind. So why do you think Jesus asked him, "What is it you want me to do for you?"

APPLY

- How do you know when someone is really listening to you? How does it make you feel? Why?

- What are some things we can do to listen to people like Jesus listened to Bartimaeus? Why is this sometimes difficult? When it's difficult, what can we do?

- How do you know Jesus listens to us today? How does it make you feel to know Jesus always listens? How can this help you be a good listener for others?

- As followers of Jesus, why do you think it's important for us to listen to others, including those who are different from us or might think differently than us?

- Who is someone God might want you to listen to this week? How will you do this?

Wrap up

Summarize the conversation, restating what you learned about B.L.E.S.S. Practice #2 *(Listen)* through the Bible story.

Pray

Share individual prayer requests and pray for one another. Pray, too, for the people you are blessing.

THANK Jesus for always listening to us, no matter who we are, where we are, what we have to say, and no matter when we might need him.

ASK the Holy Spirit to help you follow Jesus' example and be good listeners.

BIBLE STORY

Jesus Heals Bartimaeus

(Matt. 20:29-34; Mark 10:46-52; Luke 18:35-43)

Adapted from Scripture by Lisa Ferguson

After spending time in Jericho, Jesus and his disciples were leaving the city. As they walked along, a large crowd began to follow them.

Sitting near the side of the road was a blind man named Bartimaeus. He was begging people for money. When Bartimaeus heard the noisy crowd, he wondered what all the commotion was about. Since he couldn't see, he asked the people around him, "What's happening?"

"Jesus of Nazareth is passing by!" the people answered.

When Bartimaeus heard Jesus' name, he got excited and began to shout out, "Jesus, Son of David, have mercy on me!"

The people standing near Bartimaeus scolded him and told him to be quiet, but he shouted even louder, "Son of David, have mercy on me!"

Just then Jesus heard Bartimaeus' words. He stopped walking and asked for Bartimaeus to be brought to him.

"Cheer up Bartimaeus! Get to your feet! He's asking for you!" the people told him. Bartimaeus immediately tossed his cloak aside, jumped up and went to meet Jesus.

Jesus looked at Bartimaeus and asked him, "What is it you want me to do for you?"

"Teacher, I want to see," Bartimaeus answered.

Jesus had compassion on the blind man and touched his eyes, saying, "Receive your sight. Because of your faith, you are healed." Immediately, Bartimaeus was able to see. He was so happy! He began praising God.

When all the people saw this miracle, they praised God too. And Bartimaeus joined the happy crowd and began following Jesus.

MEMORY VERSE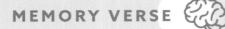

"Everyone should be quick to listen, slow to speak, and slow to become angry."

JAMES 1:19 (NIV)

Involve the whole family in memorizing the Bible verse to keep the B.L.E.S.S. practice and Bible story in your hearts and minds.

WORDS	ACTIONS
"Everyone	Open arms out in front of body
should be quick	Run in place
to listen,	Cup ears with hands
slow	Push palms down slowly in front of you
to speak,	Cup hands over mouth
and slow	Push palms down slowly in front of you
to become angry."	Clench fists
James 1:19	Form open Bible with both hands

TABLE TALK

During a meal or dessert, choose a question below for everyone to answer. Encourage everyone to respond to what is shared with comments and questions to get a conversation going around the B.L.E.S.S practice and Bible story.

☐ **Chat 1** Do you think Bartimaeus was a better listener when he was blind, or after Jesus healed him?

☐ **Chat 2** When you talk with someone, do you want them to "hear" you or "listen" to you? Is there a difference?

☐ **Chat 3** When did someone listen to you this week? What did they do or say to let you know they were really listening? How did this make you feel?

☐ **Chat 4** What do you think it means to be "quick to listen and slow to speak"? What's difficult about this? What suggestions do you have for doing this well?

☐ **Chat 5** Would others say you're better at listening or speaking? Why? What's one thing you could do to become a better listener?

☐ **Chat 6** Share a funny story about a time when you (or someone you know) thought you listened, but later realized you hadn't heard correctly.

☐ **Chat 7** What difference could it make in our home, neighborhood, school or work if we really listened to others like Jesus listened to Bartimaeus? Share examples.

☐ **Chat 8** Name one person you listened to this week. What did you learn about this person when you listened? Is there a way you can bless them, based on something they said?

The following ideas provide opportunities for you to integrate the B.L.E.S.S. practice and Bible story into your family's daily routines and experiences in fun and practical ways. Include the ideas that work best for your family and have fun blessing others together!

Do you hear what I hear?

Sit together silently inside or outside for a few moments, or take a silent walk down your block and listen carefully. Take turns sharing what you hear. Did you hear the same things? Different things? What was difficult about listening? What was enjoyable? Try this at different times of day, in different places, and see what you notice. For a challenge, sit with your eyes closed to see if it makes a difference in what you hear. Remind children what a good listener Jesus was—he was able to hear Bartimaeus' voice above the noisy crowd and find out how he could help.

Good listeners

As you notice your children listening well to you and each other, affirm them, specifically identifying what you noticed. Remind them they are being good listeners like Jesus: *"I noticed you stopped playing with your dolls and turned to look at your sister when she was talking. That helped her know you were really listening. You're being a good listener, just like Jesus was with Bartimaeus!"*

Loving your neighbor

While you run errands together, take time to strike up conversations with those who serve you: the cashier, waiter, receptionist, etc., and really listen like Jesus listened. Later, brainstorm together how you might return and bless them based on something they said (a homemade card to express sympathy, a special treat to congratulate them, or flowers to brighten their day).

Family outing

Give your ears a treat by attending a musical concert at an outdoor park or concert hall together. Or get permission to sit in the hallway of a music school, or to attend a school band or church worship team rehearsal. Take along an age-appropriate picture book of musical instruments and have fun quietly identifying the instruments you see and recognizing their sounds. For a challenge, try closing your eyes to see if you can recognize the instruments and their sounds without watching. Remind children that sharpening our listening skills will help us get better at listening to others so we can know how to bless them.

Which one doesn't belong?

Practice your listening skills by taking turns naming a place and action, four things associated with these, and one item that doesn't belong. For example: *"I went to the laundromat and I saw a dryer, a basket, a boat, laundry detergent, and people."* Listeners name the item that doesn't belong *(boat)*. For a challenge, take turns silently thinking of a category, five category-related things and one item that doesn't belong. Say these in an order that challenges listeners to guess the word that doesn't belong: *"hat, ball, bed, base, mitt, bat"* *(bed)*. Then see if they can name the category *(baseball)*.

Branches of blessings

Have you blessed someone by **listening** to them? Don't forget to add fabric strips to the branches you collected in B.L.E.S.S. Practice Toolkit #1.

WHAT'S NEXT? ───────────────→

B.L.E.S.S. PRACTICE TOOLKIT #3
EAT

EAT

CONVERSATION GUIDE

Ask a "Warm-Up" question

If you could spend time with one person and follow them around for a day, who would it be?

Read the Bible story

Before you read, pray out loud to invite the Holy Spirit's presence. Then encourage everyone to imagine the scenes in the story as they listen.

After you read, ask how the Warm-Up question connected to the Bible story. *(Matthew followed Jesus.)*

Talk about it

Use the questions below as springboards for conversation. Choose from the Reflect questions first, and then from the Apply questions.

REFLECT

- Why do you think Jesus asked Matthew to follow him, even when he knew Matthew was a cheating tax collector? Would you have asked Matthew to follow you? Why or why not?

- Why do you think Jesus went to Matthew's house for dinner, even though he knew people didn't like Matthew? Why do you think Jesus took his disciples with him?

- What do you imagine the disciples were thinking and feeling about going to Matthew's house? What do you imagine Matthew and his friends were thinking and feeling about sharing a meal with Jesus and the disciples?

- Why do you think the Jewish leaders were so upset about this dinner? What do you think about how Jesus answered their question? What do you think Jesus wanted them to know?

- In what ways do you think this special dinner with Jesus blessed Matthew and his friends? How did it bless the disciples?

APPLY

- What makes eating a meal together so special? What might be difficult about eating a meal with someone?

- What does Jesus' example teach us about eating meals with others?

- As followers of Jesus, why is it important to eat meals with others? How might it bless them? How might it bless you?

- Do you know someone like Mathew at school, work or in the neighborhood? How can you offer to share a meal with them? Who else can you invite to join you?

- Has anyone invited you or your family to share a meal recently? Reflect on this experience and past meals with others. Who can you invite to share a meal, snack or dessert with your family this week?

Wrap up

Summarize the conversation, restating what you learned about B.L.E.S.S. Practice #3 *(Eat)* through the Bible story.

Pray

Share individual prayer requests and pray for one another. Pray, too, for the people you are blessing.

THANK Jesus for showing us how sharing a meal with others can be a special way to bless them.

ASK the Holy Spirit to make you aware of opportunities to share a meal, snack or dessert with someone this week, including those you are praying for.

BIBLE STORY

Dinner at Matthew's House

(Matt. 9:9-13; Mark 2:13-17; Luke 5:27-32)

Adapted from Scripture by Lisa Ferguson

One day after Jesus taught a large crowd by the Sea of Galilee, he was walking through the town of Capernaum when he saw a man named Matthew, also called Levi, working at the local tax booth. Matthew was a Jewish man, but he worked for the Roman officials collecting money from the Jewish people to pay taxes to Rome.

The tax collectors did not have a good reputation. They often cheated the people by charging more money than the amount required and kept this stolen money for themselves. So they were very wealthy. Because of this, the Jewish people hated the tax collectors.

Knowing all this, Jesus walked right up to Matthew while he was sitting at the tax booth and said to him, "Follow me."

Immediately and eagerly, Matthew got up, left everything, and followed Jesus.

Matthew was so excited about meeting Jesus that he wanted all his friends to meet Jesus too. So he planned a special dinner at his own house and invited him.

When the Jewish leaders saw Jesus and his disciples eating dinner at Matthew's house, they asked Jesus' followers, "Why does Jesus eat and drink with tax collectors and other people who make so many wrong choices?"

When Jesus heard them talking, he said to them, "I am here for everyone who has lost their way and made wrong choices. I have come to help those who are sorry for their wrong choices to turn away from them, and turn back to God."

MEMORY VERSE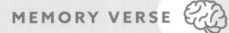

"So whether you eat or drink, or whatever you do, do it all for the glory of God."

1 CORINTHIANS 10:31 (NIV)

Involve the whole family in memorizing the Bible verse to keep the B.L.E.S.S. practice and Bible story in your hearts and minds.

WORDS	ACTIONS
"So whether you eat	Feed yourself from your palm
or drink,	Pretend to lift a glass to your mouth
or whatever	Palms facing up
you do	Fist over fist
do it all	Arms over head and then lower to sides
for the glory of God."	Wave hands over head
First Corinthians 10:31	Form open Bible with both hands

TABLE TALK

During a meal or dessert, choose a question below for everyone to answer.
Encourage everyone to respond to what is shared with comments and questions
to get a conversation going around the B.L.E.S.S practice and Bible story.

Chat 1 Would you rather ... invite guests to your house for a meal, be a guest at someone else's house for a meal, or go to a restaurant with others?

Chat 2 If Jesus came to your house for dinner, how would you feel? What would you do? What would you serve? Who would you invite?

Chat 3 How do you feel about lunchtime at school, work or home? What do you most enjoy? Least enjoy? What would make this time better?

Chat 4 Share about a time you enjoyed a special meal with someone. What made it so special? What did you learn about the other person? What did they learn about you?

Chat 5 What do you imagine it was like to have dinner at Matthew's fancy house? If you could eat somewhere fancy, where would you go? Who would you invite to join you?

Chat 6 If your friends or colleagues saw you eating lunch with someone they didn't like and were upset about it, what would you say to them? Share your experiences.

Chat 7 As followers of Jesus, how do you think eating a meal with someone brings glory (honor) to God, as the Memory Verse says?

Chat 8 Name one person with whom you shared a meal this week. How did it go? How was it a blessing to them? To you?

TOGETHER TIME 😄

The following ideas provide opportunities for you to integrate the B.L.E.S.S. practice and Bible story into your family's daily routines and experiences in fun and practical ways. Include the ideas that work best for your family and have fun blessing others together!

Good eats

Ask your child to help you come up with different categories of places to eat in your community: restaurants, coffee houses, ice cream shops, etc. Challenge them to guess which of these categories has the greatest (and fewest!) number of places in your community. As you run errands together, take the list with you and keep count of places in each category you see. Compare the tallies to your guesses—how well did you guess? How many of these places have you visited? Which places have you visited with others? What place might be fun to visit next? If you could take another family with you, who would you invite?

Look who's coming to dinner

Plan a special dinner at home with an extra chair and place setting for Jesus. Make a list of the meal ingredients you'll need, and then head to the grocery store together. Involve your children in prepping the meal, including setting a beautiful table with a tablecloth, flowers, candles, and your best dishes. (They may even want to decorate Jesus' chair!) During the meal, imagine Jesus sitting in the empty chair. What would you talk about? What might he ask you? What would you ask him? What jokes might he tell? Remind your children that Jesus is with us at every meal!

Loving your neighbor

Start a family discussion about people or families who might be fun to get to know better and then brainstorm ways to do this ... invite them over for a cookout or s'mores; or plan a time to meet at a local restaurant or donut shop. Before you invite them, pray together that they'll accept your invitation. Then pray again just before you meet ... that your time together will be honoring to God and a blessing to each other.

Family outing

Invite friends you'd like to bless to join you and your family on a visit to a local vegetable farm, farmer's market, or fruit orchard. Have fun learning about the fruits or vegetables in season, picking some and sampling them together. Return home with your friends to prepare a tasty treat, snack or an entire meal together, using the fresh ingredients you gathered.

I went to the store

Play this familiar game at home, in the car, or anywhere you find yourselves waiting, as a fun way to remember the importance of blessing others with a meal. The first person starts by saying, *"I went to the store and I bought some (food item)."* The next person repeats this phrase and adds their own food item to the list. Play continues with everyone repeating all the previous items and then adding one new food item. Go around as many times as you'd like. For a challenge, add an attribute that describes the food item (*crunchy* carrots, *tangy* tangerines, *salty* crackers, etc.).

Branches of blessings

Have you blessed someone by **eating** with them? Don't forget to add fabric strips to the branches you collected in B.L.E.S.S. Practice Toolkit #1.

WHAT'S NEXT? $\longrightarrow$

B.L.E.S.S. PRACTICE TOOLKIT #4
SERVE

SERVE

CONVERSATION GUIDE

Ask a "Warm-Up" question

If you could give up doing one thing for the rest of your life, what would it be?

Read the Bible story

Before you read, pray out loud to invite the Holy Spirit's presence. Then encourage everyone to imagine the scenes in the story as they listen.

After you read, ask how the Warm-Up question connected to the Bible story. *(Jesus did a job no one wanted to do—he washed the disciples' feet.)*

Talk about it

Use the questions below as springboards for conversation. Choose from the Reflect questions first, and then from the Apply questions.

REFLECT

- When the disciples realized there was no servant in the room, why do you think they didn't just wash their own feet? Why didn't any of them say anything about this? What would you have done?

- Why do you think there was no servant in that upper room to wash the disciples' feet? Do you think Jesus might have planned this on purpose? Why or why not?

- Why do you think Jesus washed the disciples' feet? What do you notice about when he did this? Why do you think Jesus waited so long?

- What do you think the disciples were feeling or thinking as Jesus washed their feet? How would you have reacted—like Peter, the other disciples, or in some other way?

- How might this foot-washing experience have made the disciples think or act differently toward one another? Toward others?

APPLY

- Do you think Jesus wanted his followers to really wash each other's feet, or do you think he had another idea in mind?

- What do you think it looks like to serve people like Jesus? What's difficult about this? What if we serve them, but they never notice or thank us?

- As followers of Jesus, why should we serve people who already know and love Jesus? Why might Jesus want us to serve people who don't know him yet?

- Share about a time when someone served you or your family. How was it helpful? How did it make you feel? Share your experiences of serving others. How did it bless them? How did it bless you?

- Share specific ways your family members can serve each other this week. Brainstorm how your family can serve others in your church or community, and then make plans to do so.

Wrap up

Summarize the conversation, restating what you learned about B.L.E.S.S. Practice #4 *(Serve)* through the Bible story.

Pray

Share individual prayer requests and pray for one another. Pray, too, for the people you are blessing.

THANK Jesus for teaching us what it looks like to serve others.

ASK the Holy Spirit to remind you to find ways to serve others, including the people you are praying for.

Jesus Washes the Disciples' Feet

(Matt. 26:17-19; Mark 14:12-17; Luke 22:7-13; John 13:1-15)

Adapted from Scripture by Lisa Ferguson

For three years, Jesus spent time teaching people about his Father, God, and his Father's kingdom by the Sea of Galilee in Israel. He taught them how to be generous and forgiving, sincere, and honest.

With his twelve closest disciples by his side, Jesus also did all kinds of miracles, including healing the sick and injured, and even raising some from the dead! All of these things were part of the important, rescuing work Jesus came to do.

Now Jesus was in the city of Jerusalem with his disciples for the beginning of the Passover Feast. This would be his final and most important week on earth. It would also be the most difficult. And when he completed it, he would return to his Father in heaven.

Part of the Passover celebration included a special meal of remembrance that required lots of preparation. For this meal, God had instructed the Jewish people to sacrifice a perfect lamb. This lamb was meant to remind them of the night of the "pass over," hundreds of years earlier, when their families were slaves in Egypt. On that night, God had told the Israelites to put the blood of a perfect lamb on the sides and top of the doorframe of their homes, so that the angel of death would know to "pass over" them.

So on the first day of Passover week, the disciples asked Jesus where they should go to get things ready for this special meal.

Jesus knew this would be the last time he would eat with his twelve disciples on earth, and he wanted everything to be just right. So Jesus gave Peter and John special instructions to prepare for their last supper together: "When you enter the city, look for a man carrying a jar of water. He will be there to meet you. Follow him to a certain house. When you arrive, tell the owner, 'The Teacher sent us here to find out where the guest room is, so he can eat the Passover meal with his disciples.' Then he will take you upstairs and show you a large room. Everything you need to prepare the meal will be there."

Peter and John left and found everything just as Jesus told them. So they got busy preparing for the Passover supper.

At dusk, Jesus and the other ten disciples arrived. They had been walking on the dusty roads all day, and their feet were very dirty. As they removed their sandals, they must have looked around for a servant who would come and wash their dirty feet, for that was their custom. They saw a towel, a jar of water, and a basin for washing, but no servant. So they reclined around the table without washing their feet. Before long, the meal was served.

At some point during the meal, Jesus stood up from the table and walked over to the area with the wash basin. He removed his outer layer of clothes, grabbed the towel near the basin and tied it around his waist. Then he poured the water into the basin. One by one, he began washing the disciples' feet and drying them with the towel.

When it was Simon Peter's turn, he refused to let Jesus wash his feet. But Jesus spoke gently to Peter.

"I know you don't understand what I'm doing right now, but later it will all make sense."

Peter still did not want Jesus to wash his feet: "You will never wash my feet!" Peter said.

"If I don't wash you clean," Jesus said, "you have no part with me." When Simon Peter heard these words, he stopped refusing. So Jesus washed his feet too.

When Jesus finished washing all of the disciples' feet, he put his outer layer of clothes back on and returned to his place at the table. Then he said to his disciples, "Now that I, your Lord and Teacher, have washed your feet, you should also wash one another's feet. I have done this to set an example for you so that you will do for others as I have done for you."

MEMORY VERSE ————————————————————

"For even the Son of Man did not come to be served, but to serve, and to give his life as a ransom for many."

MARK 10:45 (NIV)

Involve the whole family in memorizing the Bible verse to keep the B.L.E.S.S. practice and Bible story in your hearts and minds.

NOTE: "Son of Man" refers to Jesus.

WORDS	ACTIONS
"For even	Point up
the Son of Man	Point to middle of each palm
did not	Shake index finger "no"
come	Arms down in front of body
to be served,	Fist over fist
but to serve,	Palms facing up
and to give his life	Cross clenched fists
as a ransom	Hands cupped together
for many."	Spread hands apart
Mark 10:45	Form open Bible with hands

TABLE TALK

During a meal or dessert, choose a question below for everyone to answer. Encourage everyone to respond to what is shared with comments and questions to get a conversation going around the B.L.E.S.S practice and Bible story.

☐ **Chat 1** How do you feel about serving others? How do you feel about being the one who is served? Which do you prefer?

☐ **Chat 2** How might the world be different if everyone served one another? How might our home be different if everyone in our family served each other?

☐ **Chat 3** If Jesus came to our house to serve you or our family, what might he do? What might he want you or our family to know or do as a result?

☐ **Chat 4** Which do you think is more difficult: serving people in our family or serving people outside our family? What would make it easier?

☐ **Chat 5** Do you think serving someone after they've asked for help is the same as serving someone before they ask for help? Share your experiences.

☐ **Chat 6** Why is it sometimes difficult for people to let others serve them? Has it ever been difficult for you? What can we do when being served is difficult for us?

☐ **Chat 7** Did the Holy Spirit prompt you to serve someone this week? If so, how did you respond? How did the person you served respond?

☐ **Chat 8** How did someone serve you this week? How was this a blessing for you? For the other person?

TOGETHER TIME

The following ideas provide opportunities for you to integrate the B.L.E.S.S. practice and Bible story into your family's daily routines and experiences in fun and practical ways. Include the ideas that work best for your family and have fun blessing others together!

What great service!

As you run errands together, be on the lookout for places where people serve others (restaurants, hospitals, firehouses, etc.). How many do you see? How many people can you spot serving others (hair stylists, bus drivers, mechanics, etc.)? And don't forget to be intentional about serving others too: opening doors, picking up something that someone has dropped, letting someone go ahead of you in line, etc. Let your children know what a joy it is to serve others, like Jesus.

Service with a smile

Serving others begins at home, so encourage everyone in your family to listen and watch for opportunities to serve one another: do a sibling's chore, take a glass of lemonade to dad, set the table without being asked, etc. As your children serve, let them know how their acts of service are a blessing to each of you, and to your whole family. (You might even plan a special time to wash one another's feet, using small containers of warm, sudsy water as you imagine Jesus washing the disciples' feet.)

Loving your neighbor

Is someone in your neighborhood ill? Elderly? Going on vacation? Listen and watch for opportunities to serve your neighbors. Brainstorm ways you can offer to serve them as a family: walking a pet, watering flowers, getting mail, etc. Be sure to involve each family member in some way. Afterward, reflect on your experience serving together as a way to bless others and honor Jesus.

Family outing

Find out about opportunities to serve as a family at church (as greeters, in children's ministry, on the baking team, etc.) and with organizations in your community (a food pantry, homeless shelter, after-school program, etc.). Present ideas your family can choose from and then set a date to volunteer. Afterward, reflect together on your experience serving and blessing others. Consider making this a regular family activity and inviting other families to join you. Staying connected to your church or the organization will help you build relationships and find ways to keep serving and blessing others all year.

Charades

Create two "fair" teams and secretly brainstorm eight to ten creative ways to "serve" others: raking leaves, rocking a baby, walking a dog, etc. Write each of these on a strip of paper and place them in a basket. Exchange baskets. One person from the first team chooses a strip and acts out what it says, without talking, while their teammate(s) guesses the action. Next, someone from the second team chooses a strip to act out. Play continues, with each team taking turns until every strip has been acted out. With each round, switch the "actor" and "guesser(s)." If someone needs a hint, the "actor" can name the context (in the kitchen, outside, etc.). Older children may enjoy using a timer and keeping score. After you play, talk about which of these activities you did this week to serve others and which ones you might do to serve others in the future.

Branches of blessings

Have you blessed someone by **serving** them? Don't forget to add fabric strips to the branches you collected in B.L.E.S.S. Practice Toolkit #1.

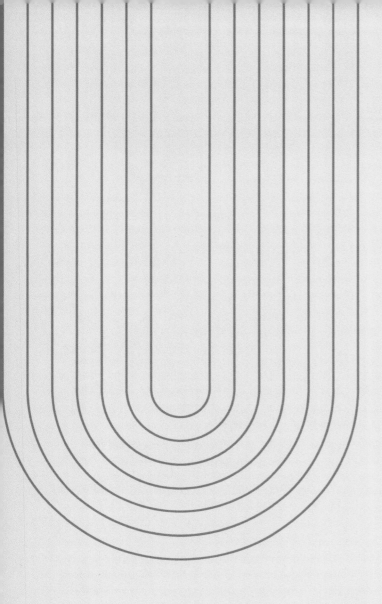

WHAT'S NEXT? ————————————→

STORY

CONVERSATION GUIDE

Ask a "Warm-Up" question

Would you rather go to a beach or a pool?

Read the Bible story

Before you read, pray out loud to invite the Holy Spirit's presence. Then encourage everyone to imagine the scenes in the story as they listen.

After you read, ask how the Warm-Up question connected to the Bible story. *(Jesus told the blind man to wash in the Pool of Siloam.)*

Talk about it

Use the questions below as springboards for conversation. Choose from the Reflect questions first, and then from the Apply questions.

REFLECT

- Why do you think the disciples thought that wrong choices ("sins") had caused the man to be blind? What do you think about Jesus' response? How did his words come true?

- Why do you think Jesus put mud on the blind man's eyes and then told him to wash in a public pool? How was this an important part of his story?

- The healed man had the opportunity to share his story many times. How might this have been helpful for him? For others?

- Why do you think the Jewish leaders asked to hear the man's story so many times? Why did they refuse to believe him? Would you have believed him? Why or why not?

- What do you imagine this man's life was like before he met Jesus? After he met Jesus? After he met Jesus the second time? How do you think his story made others want to know and follow Jesus?

APPLY

- Why do you think it's important to share our stories with others about how Jesus has worked in our lives? How is this helpful for us? For others? What's difficult about this?

- If you were asked to share a story about how Jesus worked in your life or your family's life, what would you share?

- What can you learn from the blind man that will help you share your story with others?

- Why is it sometimes difficult to believe people's stories about how Jesus has worked in their lives? What can we do when we share our story, but people don't believe us?

- With whom have you shared your story about how you came to know Jesus? Who has shared their story with you? Share your experiences.

Wrap up

Summarize the conversation, restating what you learned about B.L.E.S.S. Practice #5 (*Story*) through the Bible story.

Pray

Share individual prayer requests and pray for one another. Pray, too, for the people you are blessing.

THANK Jesus for working so personally in each of our lives and allowing our stories to help others know how much he loves them.

ASK the Holy Spirit to give you opportunities to share your story with others in a powerful way so that they may choose to follow Jesus.

Jesus Heals a Man Born Blind

(John 9:1-38)

Adapted from Scripture by Lisa Ferguson

One day as Jesus and his disciples were taking a walk, they saw a man who was blind. He had been blind his whole life, since he was born. The disciples asked Jesus, "Teacher, whose wrong choices made this man blind? Was it the man's own wrong choices, or his parents'?"

Jesus told them: "This man is not blind because of his or his parents' sins, but to demonstrate the work of God in his life."

Then Jesus spit on the ground, mixed some dirt with his saliva and made mud. He spread this mud on the man's eyes. "Go to the Pool of Siloam and wash yourself," Jesus told the man. So the man obeyed Jesus. As he was washing, he rubbed off the mud. When he opened his eyes, he could see for the very first time!

When the man's neighbors saw him, they were confused. "Isn't this the man who used to sit by the road, begging for money?" they asked. "Yes! He's the man!" some said.

But others disagreed. "He just looks like him," they said.

When the man heard them talking, he spoke up, "It's me! I am the man who was blind and begging."

"Then how are you able to see?" they asked him.

Then the man shared his story: "The man named Jesus made some mud, put it on my eyes and told me to go wash in the Pool of Siloam. So I did. And when I opened my eyes, I could see!"

"Where is this man named Jesus?" they asked.

"I don't know," said the man.

Some people brought the healed man to the Jewish leaders so he could share his story with them. When some of the leaders, also called the Pharisees, heard that Jesus had healed the man by putting mud on his eyes on the Sabbath, they became angry.

"He put mud on your eyes? That is work! The Sabbath is a day to rest—no work is allowed. This man cannot be from God because he did not follow the law of the Sabbath," some said.

Other leaders were confused and asked, "How could a man do such a miracle if he is not from God?"

When the Pharisees still did not believe the man had been blind or that Jesus had healed his eyes, they sent for the man's parents to hear their story.

"He's definitely our son and we can tell you for sure that he's been blind since the day he was born," his parents explained. "But we have no idea how he can now see, or who healed him. He's old enough to tell you what happened for himself. Why don't you ask him?" The man's parents were afraid. They had heard that the Pharisees had made a rule that anyone who believed Jesus was the Messiah—the Promised Rescuer sent by God—would not be allowed to worship in the synagogue.

When the leaders asked the man to come in to share his story a second time, the man said, "I don't know much about the man who healed me, but what I do know for sure is that I used to be blind, but now I can see!"

Then they asked him, "What did the man named Jesus do to give you your sight? How did he heal your eyes?"

"I already told you, but you didn't listen to me," the man said. "Why do you want me to share my story again? Do you want to follow him too?"

When the Jewish leaders heard this, they became very angry. They said mean and hurtful things to the healed man: "We follow Moses because we know God spoke to him. As for the man who healed you, we know nothing about him, not even where he comes from!"

"Now that's amazing!" the healed man said. "You know nothing about him but yet he healed my eyes so I can see. No one has ever heard of healing the eyes of a man born blind."

The leaders were angry with the man's words, so they threw him out of the synagogue.

Later, Jesus found the healed man and helped him know that he really was the Messiah, God's own son, the Promised Rescuer of the world.

The man believed and worshiped Jesus.

MEMORY VERSE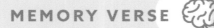

"Always be prepared to give an answer to everyone who asks you to give the reason for the hope that you have."

1 PETER 3:15 (NIV)

Involve the whole family in memorizing the Bible verse to keep the B.L.E.S.S. practice and Bible story in your hearts and minds.

WORDS	ACTIONS
"Always	Point index finger up and circle around
be prepared	Hold hands together in front of body
to give an answer	Cup hands over mouth
to everyone	Open arms out in front of body
who asks you	Cup hand over ear
to give the reason	Point to temple
for the hope	Wave both hands over head
that you have."	Hands over heart
First Peter 3:15	Form open Bible with hands

During a meal or dessert, choose a question below for everyone to answer.
Encourage everyone to respond to what is shared with comments and questions
to get a conversation going around the B.L.E.S.S practice and Bible story.

Chat 1 Do you prefer make-believe (fiction) stories or true (non-fiction) stories? How can a true story about God at work in someone's life make a difference in your own life?

Chat 2 What's the first story you remember hearing about Jesus? Who shared it with you? Where were you? What do you remember about it? How did it make you feel?

Chat 3 What does it mean to be blind? Is it possible that someone who can see with their eyes might be "blind" in other ways?

Chat 4 If someone asked you to share your favorite story about Jesus (other than his birth and resurrection), which one would you share? Why is it your favorite?

Chat 5 How can we know when to share our story with someone about how Jesus has worked in our lives and when to listen to someone else's story? Share your experiences.

Chat 6 When people come to know and love Jesus, they sometimes say, "I was blind, but now I see." What do you think they mean? Have you ever felt this way? Share your experience.

Chat 7 Have you ever heard or read someone's story that helped you understand something new about God or a relationship with Jesus? Explain.

Chat 8 What stories from your immediate and/or extended family remind you of God's love and faithfulness?

TOGETHER TIME 😄

The following ideas provide opportunities for you to integrate the B.L.E.S.S. practice and Bible story into your family's daily routines and experiences in fun and practical ways. Include the ideas that work best for your family and have fun blessing others together!

What's the story?

Whenever you find yourselves waiting, look around for art (paintings, photos, flower arrangements, textiles, murals, sculptures or even an interesting object or building). Talk about the story the artist may have wanted to communicate through their work. Let your children know that in a similar way, God is the artist working through each of us so we can have our own story to share about the difference he makes in our lives.

Heroes and heroines

Be inspired by the stories of contemporary people who made a difference for Jesus. Learn their stories by checking out an age-appropriate book, audiobook, or movie together. Reflect on how God worked through their story to help others come to know Jesus. *(Examples: Billy Graham, Martin Luther, Dr. Martin Luther King, Jr., Eric Liddell, George Washington Carver, Corrie ten Boom, Jim and Elisabeth Elliot, Harriet Tubman, William Wilberforce, William and Catherine Booth, Mother Theresa, Luís Palau, Joni Eareckson Tada, etc.).*

Loving your neighbor

As you build relationships with others by **B**eginning with prayer, **L**istening, **E**ating together, and **S**erving, your family may eventually have the opportunity to share your **S**tory of the difference Jesus makes in your lives. When this happens, what story will you share? Take time to think about this together. Ask everyone to write their own individual stories and then practice telling them to one another (parents can write as children dictate). Keep it brief and to the point. Think in terms of the beginning *(before your relationship with Jesus)*, middle *(meeting Jesus and understanding what his death and resurrection means to you personally)* and end *(growing in your relationship with Jesus and being confident*

you will be with him in heaven one day). As you find opportunities to share your personal stories with others, don't forget to invite them to your church so they can hear more stories about Jesus and discover the difference he can make in their lives too!

Family outing

Research local memorials, monuments, tombs, museums or childhood homes that honor the memory of someone who made a positive difference in the world. Make plans to visit one of these locations and learn the story behind it. You could also stop by the home or other special place of a friend or family member, past or present, whose story you'd like to pass on to your children. Talk about their story and the difference it made in the lives of others.

String-along story

Experience the fun and power of a good story. First, decide on the kind of story you'd like to tell: silly, a fairy tale, a retelling of a familiar story or family experience, etc. Then have the first person begin with, "Once upon a time …" The next person adds a line, then the next, and so on. Go around as many times as you'd like. When done, talk about what makes a story "good." Remind your children that we all have good stories to share about God's good work in our lives.

Branches of blessings

Have you blessed someone by sharing your **story** with them about your friendship with Jesus? Don't forget to add fabric strips to the branches you collected in B.L.E.S.S. Practice Toolkit #1.

As you wrap up this series, take time to admire the branches and reflect on your experiences blessing others. Keep the branches on display as a reminder to continue blessing the people around you.

WHAT'S NEXT? ⟶

FOUR GREAT WAYS TO USE
THE B.L.E.S.S. FAMILY RESOURCE

FOUR GREAT WAYS TO USE

THE B.L.E.S.S. FAMILY RESOURCE

Two Plans for Families

6-WEEK PLAN

Choose a day and time to meet each week, for six weeks. During the first five weeks, read aloud the Bible stories using the Conversation Guides included in each Toolkit. When you make this an enjoyable part of your family's weekly routine, your children will look forward to this special time with you.

Meeting early in the week will give you time to try the Memory Verse, Table Talk questions and Together Time activities in each Toolkit. Include these in ways that work best for your family. For example, you might choose to ask a Table Talk question at dinner each night or at breakfast one morning. You may build a Together Time activity into your daily routine or make plans to do one on a Saturday. The goal is to keep the practices and Bible stories alive in your home in fun and meaningful ways for everyone.

In the sixth week, use the Closing Conversation Guide at the back of this resource (p. 37) to wrap up the series and reflect on your learning as a family. Celebrate all you've learned about blessing others with a fun treat or dessert.

21-WEEK PLAN

Follow the 4-Week Cycle on the next page to explore the five B.L.E.S.S. practices over twenty weeks. Utilize the Memory Verse, Table Talk questions and Together Time activities in each Toolkit to keep the practice alive over all four weeks. In the twenty-first week, use the Closing Conversation Guide (p. 37) to wrap up the series and reflect on your learning as a family. Celebrate all you've learned about blessing others with a fun treat or dessert.

Two Plans for Small Groups of Families

6-WEEK PLAN

With this plan, a small group of families will meet once a week for six weeks. During the first five weeks, the group will explore one B.L.E.S.S. practice and Bible story each meeting. Parents can take turns facilitating these group discussions using the

Conversation Guides and Bible stories included in each of the five Toolkits. During the series, the group may also choose to adapt one of the Together Time activities and make plans to experience it collectively. In the sixth week, they can wrap up the series and celebrate their learning with family presentations, reflections and a special treat.

At Home

In the days before and after the weekly group meetings, families can begin and end the conversations at home using two additional conversation guides found at the back of this resource (First Impressions and Reflections). They can also try the Memory Verse, Table Talk questions and Together Time activities listed in each Toolkit as their schedule permits.

Weekly Format

At Home: First Impressions Conversation Guide
            (p. 35)

In Group: Conversation Guide (in each Toolkit)

At Home: Reflections Conversation Guide
            (p. 36)

6th Week - Celebration of Learning

Several days before the last group meeting, families can choose one of the following ideas to present their overall learning to the entire group. Encourage them to be creative, include every member of the family, and practice before the presentation.

- A commercial for *The B.L.E.S.S. Family Resource* to inspire other families to try it

- The three most important things they learned through this entire series

- Three family goals to continue the five practices

- Act out the five practices in five minutes or less

At the final group meeting, each family will make their presentation. Pause after each presentation to let the "audience" make encouraging comments and ask questions. Then follow the Closing Conversation Guide (p. 37) to reflect on your learning through this entire series. Conclude by celebrating with a special treat or dessert.

21-WEEK PLAN

With this plan, a small group of families will gradually explore and apply the five B.L.E.S.S. practices together over twenty weeks, *focusing on one practice and Bible story every four weeks.* Parents can take turns facilitating these group discussions using the Conversation Guides and Bible stories found in each Toolkit, as well as two additional conversation guides found at the back of this resource (First Impressions and Reflections). The last week of each month, the group can adapt one of the Together Time activities for that practice and experience it collectively. In the twenty-first week, the group will wrap up the series and celebrate their learning with family presentations, reflections and a special treat.

4-Week Cycle for Each B.L.E.S.S. Practice

Week 1:   First Impressions (p. 35)

Week 2:   Conversation Guide (in each Toolkit)

Week 3:   Reflections (p. 36)

Week 4:   Together Time Activity
            (in each Toolkit)

At Home

In between group gatherings, families can utilize the Memory Verse, Table Talk questions and Together Time activities in each Toolkit to keep the practice alive over all four weeks.

21st Week - Celebration of Learning

Several days before the last group meeting, families can choose one of the following ideas to present their overall learning to the entire group. Encourage them to be creative, include every member of the family, and practice before the presentation.

- A commercial for *The B.L.E.S.S. Family Resource* to inspire other families to try it

- The three most important things they learned through this entire series

- Three family goals to continue the five practices

- Act out the five practices in five minutes or less

At the final group meeting, each family will make their presentation. Pause after each presentation to let the "audience" make encouraging comments and ask questions. End your time together using the Closing Conversation Guide (p. 37) to reflect on your learning through this entire series. Conclude by celebrating with a special treat or dessert.

10 Helpful Tips for Small Group Settings

1. Eat a meal together at the beginning of your meetings. As you eat, share your experiences blessing others and being blessed.

2. Begin your meetings with one or two worship songs. Someone who plays the guitar could lead this; or play a worship song on a cell phone and sing together.

3. Use the conversation guides to facilitate interactive conversations that include all participants, children and adults, just as you would for an adult small group.

4. To keep everyone engaged and the conversation moving, after someone shares, ask if others had the same thought, if someone would like to "build on" what was said, and if anyone disagrees with what was said and would like to explain.

5. To keep the "Warm-Up" question brief, use the "turn and talk" strategy: ask everyone to turn to someone sitting next to them and share their answer to the question. After a few moments, ask just a few to share their partner's response with the whole group. You can also use this strategy for one or two key questions during the conversation.

6. If you'd like to act out the Bible story, it's best to do so for the final reading when everyone is very familiar with it. Designate a "stage" area and determine roles. Include some parents and children as actors, while others can be the audience. One fluent reader can read the story aloud "off stage" while the actors dramatize it— no props or practice needed.

7. Options for the prayer time include praying in groups of individual families, asking one person from each family to say a sentence prayer, or having one person (parent or child) pray for the entire group.

8. End your meetings by reciting the Memory Verse together, or invite individual families to recite it to the whole group.

9. Plan ahead for your group to experience the Together Time activities. Adapt as needed.

10. Set a time limit for each family presentation during the Celebration of Learning. Add 5 minutes in between presentations for comments and questions from the audience.

WHAT'S NEXT? ————————————————→

ADDITIONAL
CONVERSATION GUIDES

FIRST IMPRESSIONS

CONVERSATION GUIDE

This is a gentle and simple way to introduce the Bible story in each B.L.E.S.S. Practice Toolkit. This first reading will allow listeners to immerse themselves in the Bible story before thinking more deeply about it in the next reading. See the preceding section titled "Four Great Ways to Use *The B.L.E.S.S. Family Resource*" for details.

Read aloud the title of the Bible story

Ask a "Warm-Up" question

Choose one question below and invite each person to respond briefly.

- What do you think this Bible story will be about? (If this is a familiar Bible story, ask each person to name one thing they remember about it.)

- What's one thought that comes to mind when you hear the title of this Bible story?

- What does the title of this Bible story remind you of? A person? A place? A past experience? Something you've read or heard before?

- What does the title of this Bible story make you wonder about?

Read the Bible story

Before you read, pray out loud to invite the Holy Spirit's presence. Then encourage everyone to imagine the scenes in the story as they listen.

Talk about it

Use some of the questions below as springboards for conversation.

- What's something you noticed in this Bible story?

- What surprised you?

- How did this story make you feel?

- How did you feel at the beginning of the story? the middle? the end?

- What came to your mind as I was reading?

- Did this story remind you of anyone (or anything, anyplace, or any situation)?

- What does this story make you wonder about?

- What question(s) do you have about this story?

- What do you think this story has to do with blessing others?

Wrap up

Let children know you're excited to re-read this Bible story and see what new things God has to teach all of you about blessing others.

Pray

Share individual prayer requests and pray for one another. Pray, too, for the people God will put in your path to bless throughout this series, including people in your neighborhood, family, at school and work.

THANK God for all you will learn through this Bible story—about God, his Son Jesus, the Holy Spirit, and blessing others.

ASK the Holy Spirit to open your eyes, ears, hearts, and minds to all that God desires for you to know and do through this Bible story to be a blessing to others.

REFLECTIONS
CONVERSATION GUIDE

Use this guide for the final reading of the Bible story in each B.L.E.S.S. Practice Toolkit. This conversation will encourage you to reflect thoughtfully on each practice before moving on to the next one. See the preceding section titled "Four Great Ways to Use *The B.L.E.S.S. Family Resource*" for details.

Ask a "Warm-Up" question

Choose one question below and invite each person to respond briefly.

- What was your favorite part of the Bible story?

- If you could ask one person from this story one question, who would you ask and what would you ask them?

- Which person in this story is most like you? Least like you?

- If you could be in this story, who would you like to be (besides Jesus)?

Share the Bible story

Now that you're all familiar with the Bible story, try sharing it in a creative way (see ideas below). Before you begin, pray out loud to invite the Holy Spirit's presence.

- Read the Bible story, omitting a few key words for others to say aloud

- Re-tell the Bible story from memory, each person adding a sentence, until the end

- One person reads the Bible story while others act it out (no props or practice needed!)

Talk about it

Use some of the questions below as springboards for conversation.

- What would you tell someone who was about to read this Bible story?

- What's one question you have about this story?

- What challenged your thinking?

- What do you feel has been the most important thing you've learned personally through this story?

- What's something you want to remember?

- How did the Holy Spirit remind you of this story? Share the circumstances.

- What do you think God wants you to know about him? About his Son, Jesus? The Holy Spirit? Other people?

- Is there anything you feel God might want you or your family to do differently after reading this story?

- How has this story made you think differently about people who don't know Jesus?

- How did this story help you and/or your family bless others in a new way? Share your stories.

Wrap up

Summarize the conversation, restating what you learned about this B.L.E.S.S. practice (*Begin with prayer, Listen, Eat, Serve, Story*) through the Bible story.

Pray

Share individual prayer requests and pray for one another. Pray, too, for the people you are blessing.

THANK God for all the things (...) you've learned through this Bible story.

ASK the Holy Spirit to help you remember what you learned and to continue to look for opportunities to apply the B.L.E.S.S. practice (*Begin with prayer, Listen, Eat, Serve, Story*) at home, school and work—and with the people you're praying for.

CLOSING

CONVERSATION GUIDE

Use this guide to reflect on your overall experience with *The B.L.E.S.S. Family Resource*. See the preceding section titled "Four Great Ways to Use *The B.L.E.S.S. Family Resource*" for details.

Talk about it

Use the questions below as springboards for conversation. Choose from the Reflect questions first, and then from the Apply questions.

PRACTICE	BIBLE STORY
Begin with prayer	*Jesus Chooses the Twelve Apostles*
Listen	*Jesus Heals Bartimaeus*
Eat	*Dinner at Matthew's House*
Serve	*Jesus Washes the Disciples' Feet*
Story	*Jesus Heals a Man Born Blind*

REFLECT

- What have you enjoyed most about blessing others?

- What's one thing from this B.L.E.S.S. series you wish you could do again?

- Which Bible story conversation was the most meaningful to you? Explain.

- Was there a particular example of blessing someone that stands out for you?

- Which of the five B.L.E.S.S. practices do you think is the most important?

- What's the most important thing you've learned about blessing others?

- What's the most important thing you and/or your family have learned about blessing others?

- What's been challenging about blessing others?

- How has this series changed how you feel, think or act toward others? *(I used to ... Now I ...)*

- How has this series changed how your family feels, thinks or acts toward others? *(We used to ... Now we ...)*

- Think about the people you've been praying for throughout this series. How has blessing them made a difference in their lives? In your life? How is it helping them know Jesus?

APPLY

- What's one thing you want to remember from the B.L.E.S.S. series?

- How can you continue to keep the five B.L.E.S.S. practices alive to help others experience the love of Jesus?

- What advice would you give to someone who wanted to bless people using the five B.L.E.S.S. practices?

- If another family was interested in using *The B.L.E.S.S. Family Resource*, what would you tell them?

Wrap up

Summarize the conversation, restating what you learned through this entire series about the five B.L.E.S.S. practices.

Pray

Share individual prayer requests and pray for one another. Give updates on the people you are blessing and pray for them too.

THANK God for all the things you've learned through this entire series.

ASK the Holy Spirit to open the hearts and minds of the people you are blessing so they will come to know Jesus. Ask God to help you keep applying the five B.L.E.S.S. practices at home, in your neighborhood, at school and at work to help more people love and follow Jesus.

About the author

Lisa Ferguson

For more than twenty-five years, Lisa has served as an early childhood education professional, focusing on language and literacy, math development and play. As a classroom teacher, professional development facilitator, coach, university instructor, mentor, and conference presenter, Lisa has worked with administrators, teachers and parents across the country. In addition, she has served in various capacities in children's ministry from volunteer to Director with Community Christian Church where she developed and launched an innovative Bible curriculum inspired by schools in Italy. She was also a homeschool educator to her two children, who are now young adults.

Lisa currently works at the Erikson Institute, specializing in professional development for early childhood administrators and teachers. She is an author of *Bringing Baby Home*, in partnership with the Illinois Department of Public Health and the Chicago Mayor's Office. Lisa also serves on the board of Reach Out and Read Illinois and is a member of the North American Reggio Emilia Alliance (NAREA).

Lisa received a bachelor's degree from Moody Bible Institute and a Master of Arts in Teaching in Early Childhood Education from National-Louis University. She lives in Chicago with her husband, Jon, co-founding pastor of Community Christian Church.

To connect with Lisa for consulting, training, and coaching, visit www.sonburst.info.

Printed in Great Britain
by Amazon

37694155R00027